KV-191-603

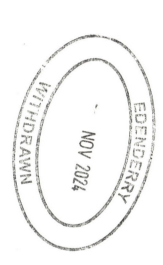

WITHDRAWN
EDENDERRY
NOV 2024

OFFALY LIBRARY

30013005538224

Bertrams   23/08/2019

DC

Smithsonian

LITTLE EXPLORER

AMAZING ANTS

Megan Cooley Peterson

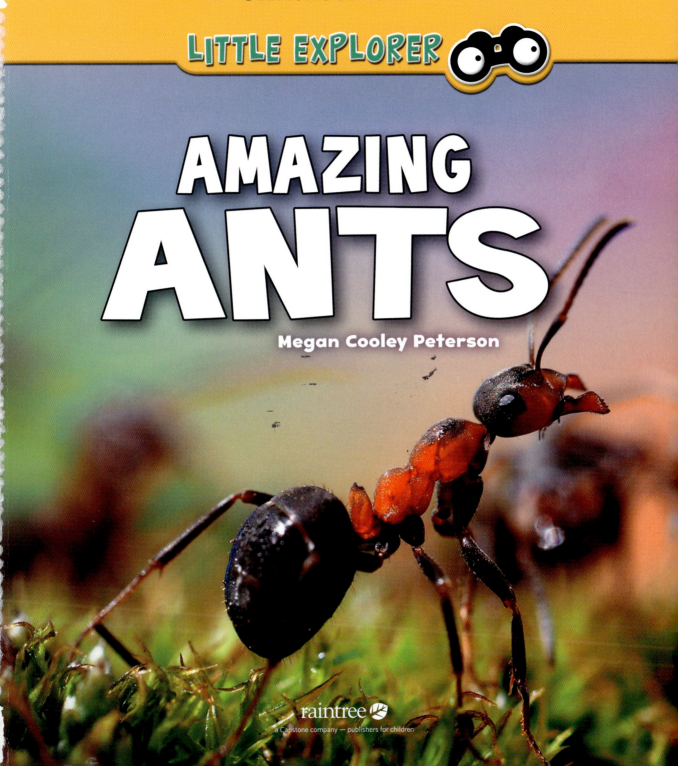

raintree
a Capstone company — publishers for children

Raintree is an imprint of Capstone Global Library Limited, a
company incorporated in England and Wales having its registered
office at 264 Banbury Road, Oxford, OX2 7DY Registered
company number: 6695582

www.raintree.co.uk
myorders@raintree.co.uk

Text © Capstone Global Library Limited 2020
The moral rights of the proprietor have been asserted.

All rights reserved. No part of this publication may be reproduced
in any form or by any means (including photocopying or storing it
in any medium by electronic means and whether or not transiently
or incidentally to some other use of this publication) without the
written permission of the copyright owner, except in accordance
with the provisions of the Copyright, Designs and Patents Act
1988 or under the terms of a licence issued by the Copyright
Licensing Agency, Barnard's Inn, 86 Fetter Lane, London, EC4A
1EN (www.cla.co.uk). Applications for the copyright owner's
written permission should be addressed to the publisher.

The name of the Smithsonian Institution and the sunburst
logo are registered trademarks of the Smithsonian Institution.
For more information, please visit www.si.edu.

Edited by Abby Colich
Designed by Kyle Grenz
Original illustrations © Capstone Global Library Limited 2020
Picture research by Kelly Garvin
Production by Tori Abraham
Originated by Capstone Global Library Ltd
Printed and bound in India

ISBN 978 1 4747 7056 9 (hardback)
ISBN 978 1 4747 7062 0 (paperback)
23 22 21 20 19
10 9 8 7 6 5 4 3 2 1

British Library Cataloguing in Publication Data
A full catalogue record for this book is available from the British
Library.

Acknowledgements
We would like to thank the following for permission to reproduce
photographs: Alamy/Universal Images Group North America,
11 (right inset); Minden Pictures: Mark Moffett, 8, Mitsuhiko
Imamori/Nature Production, 27; Nature Picture Library: Doug
Wechsler, 23, Emanuele Biggi, 13, Jurgen Freund, 17, Kim Taylor,
15; Newscom/Julio Cortez/Rapport Press, 11; Shutterstock:
aekikuis, 9, Amelia Martin, 7, Andrey Pavlov, cover, 5 (bottom
inset), Dr Morley Read, 21, 29, Hugh Lansdown, 19, Irina Kozorog,
1, Janfe, 14, Klimek Pavol, 5, Marut Khrueahong, 25, NNphotos,
18, Potapov Alexander, 2.

Our very special thanks to Gary Hevel, Public Information Officer
(Emeritus), Entomology Department, at the Smithsonian National
Museum of Natural History. Capstone would also like to thank
Kealy Gordon, Product Development Manager, and the following at
Smithsonian Enterprises: Ellen Nanney, Licensing Manager; Brigid
Ferraro, Vice President, Education and Consumer Products; and Carol
LeBlanc, Senior Vice President, Education and Consumer Products.

Every effort has been made to contact copyright holders of
material reproduced in this book. Any omissions will be rectified in
subsequent printings if notice is given to the publisher.

All the internet addresses (URLs) given in this book were valid at
the time of going to press. However, due to the dynamic nature
of the internet, some addresses may have changed, or sites may
have changed or ceased to exist since publication. While the author
and publisher regret any inconvenience this may cause readers, no
responsibility for any such changes can be accepted by either the
author or the publisher.

Contents

Meet
the ants!

Have you ever seen ants outside? They were probably hard at work. These tiny insects scurry along pavements and crawl up trees. They turn the soil, which helps plants to grow. Some ants carry seeds to underground nests. The seeds grow into new plants. Nature would be lost without ants!

There are more than 13,400 species of ants on Earth. Ants are very social. They work together to build nests, find food and keep each other safe.

DID YOU KNOW?

Only the queen and male ants have wings.

An ant's body

An ant is an insect. It has six legs and two antennae. It uses its mandibles like teeth.

eye

antennae

mandibles

legs

legs

5

Carpenter ants

Number of species: more than 1,000
Found: worldwide except Antarctica
Length: 0.5 to 2 centimetres (0.2 to 0.8 inches)

Carpenter ants build nests out of wood. That's how they got their name. These tiny builders make nests in tree trunks and branches. They even build nests inside the wood in buildings. Carpenter ants don't eat the wood. They eat other insects. They also eat some of the food people eat, such as syrup, honey and jam.

DID YOU KNOW?

Some queens lay millions of eggs a year. A colony can have just one or several queens.

Life with ants

Ants live in groups called colonies. Each ant in a colony has a job. The queen lays eggs. Male ants mate with the queen. Then they die. All females are workers. They take care of the queen and the young. They also gather food and build nests.

This carpenter ant is covered in the goo that has killed it and the enemy. The rest of the colony is now safe.

An ant's life

Ants begin life as eggs. The eggs hatch into larvae. The larvae moult as they grow. Then they spin a cocoon as pupae. The pupae emerge from the cocoon as adults.

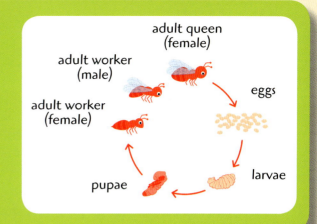

adult queen (female)

adult worker (male)

adult worker (female)

eggs

larvae

pupae

Some carpenter ants protect themselves in unusual ways. The exploding ant squeezes itself until it blows up. Yellow goo shoots out of its body. The goo sticks to predators. The predators die. The black carpenter ant bites enemies. It sprays acid into the bite mark. The acid makes the bite mark burn.

DID YOU KNOW?

Ants have thicker muscles than other insects and larger animals. These muscles help them to carry 10 to 50 times their own weight. This would be like you lifting a car over your head!

Fire ants

Number of species: about 200
Found: worldwide except Antarctica
Length: 0.3 to 1 centimetres (0.1 to 0.4 inches)

You'll know if a fire ant stings you. It burns like fire! These ants use sharp mandibles to bite into prey. Then they inject venom with stingers.

Fire ant colonies can survive a flood. They make themselves into rafts! The ants join together. They float on the water's surface. Worker ants form the outside of the raft. The queen and young stay safe on the inside.

DID YOU KNOW?

Fire ants build mounds of soil on top of their nests. Mounds can reach 60 centimetres (2 feet) tall.

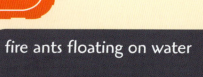
fire ants floating on water

Inside a nest

Most ants build their nests in soil. Some ants build nests in trees or in people's homes. Workers dig tunnels and rooms, called chambers. The queen lives in her own chamber. Workers use other chambers. They store food or care for the young in these chambers.

Turtle ants

Number of species: more than 100
Found: Central and South America, southern United States
Length: 0.5 to 2.3 centimetres (0.2 to 0.9 inches)

It's moving day for turtle ants. These ants don't build their own nests. Instead, they look for an empty beetle burrow in a tree. Once the ants move in, workers use their heads like doors. Their large heads block the opening of the nest.

Quiet ants

Ants don't make noise. They communicate by releasing chemicals. Each species uses 10 to 20 different chemicals. When an ant finds food, it releases a chemical. Other ants follow it to the food. Another chemical is used to warn the colony of danger.

Turtle ants have a daring way of getting to the bottom of a tree. They jump! A turtle ant's flattened body and legs help it to steer and glide. It lands at the bottom of the tree.

turtle ant's head

Wood ants

Number of species: about 200
Found: Europe, the Middle East and North America
Length: 0.5 to 1.3 centimetres (0.2 to 0.5 inches)

Most wood ants live in wooded areas or fields. They build large mounds on top of underground nests. The mounds soak up the sunlight. The sun's heat keeps the colony warm.

DID YOU KNOW?

Some wood ant mounds can reach 2.1 metres (7 feet) tall. Scientists once found 1,400 queens inside a single mound.

Wood ants have a trick to scare away predators. Workers spray acid at them. The predators run from the foul liquid.

Giant Amazonian ants

Number of species: 6
Found: South America
Length: up to 4.1 centimetres (1.6 inches)

In South America a giant creature crawls along the forest floor. The giant Amazonian ant is one of the largest ants on Earth. Most of these ants live in small colonies.

The dinosaur ant is a type of giant Amazonian ant. Between 40 and 100 workers live in a colony. They build their nests at the base of trees. Their strong mandibles chomp down on prey. They also inject venom with stingers.

DID YOU KNOW?
Giant Amazonian ant colonies don't have queens. Worker ants lay eggs.

Weaver ants

Number of species: 2
Found: Africa, Australia and Asia
Length: 0.5 to 2.5 centimetres (0.2 to 1 inches)

Weaver ants enjoy a room with a view. High in the treetops, they build nests out of leaves. Workers hold the edges of leaves together. Other workers pass larvae back and forth. The larvae spit out silk. The silk "sews" the leaf edges together. Each colony builds 6 to 100 nests. A single weaver ant nest is about the size of a football.

weaver ant nest

DID YOU KNOW?

Weaver ants make themselves into bridges. They climb over each other to close the gap between distant leaves or branches.

Leaf-cutter ants

Number of species: 39
Found: North and South America
Length: 0.3 to 1.8 centimetres (0.1 to 0.7 inches)

Leaf-cutter ants grow their own food. At night, workers leave their huge underground nests. They use their sharp mandibles to cut pieces of leaves from trees and shrubs. The mandibles vibrate a thousand times per second as they cut the leaves. The workers chew the leaves into a pulp. They use the pulp to grow fungus inside the nest, which they eat.

DID YOU KNOW?

Leaf-cutter ant queens can live for 25 years or more. When the queen dies, the other ants in the colony die too.

Acrobat ants

Number of species: about 490
Found: worldwide except Antarctica
Length: 0.3 to 0.8 centimetres (0.1 to 0.3 inches)

Acrobat ants know how to put on a show! These ants have bodies shaped like hearts. When threatened, the ants lift up their bodies. To enemies the ants look bigger. The ants look like acrobats as they walk.

Acrobat ants live in trees. They build nests in damp or rotting wood. Some build carton nests. Carton nests look like cardboard. The ants chew up plants and mix them with soil to build the nests. Carton nests may have many tunnels and chambers.

Acrobat ants eat the waste of smaller insects.

For every human, there are 1.5 million ants. The weight of all people on Earth is equal to the weight of all ants.

Crazy ants

Number of species: about 123
Found: Worldwide except Europe and Antarctica
Length: 0.1 to 0.5 centimetres (0.04 to 0.2 inches)

Watch out for crazy ants! These ants dash and dart in all directions. They kill other ants that get in their way. They even crawl onto people's shoes and up their legs. Crazy ants spray acid at other animals and people. It makes their prey's skin and eyes sting.

One type of crazy ant takes over places where fire ants live. The crazy ants cover themselves with their own acid. It protects them from fire ant venom.

DID YOU KNOW?

Crazy ants invade people's homes. Sometimes they build nests inside computers and TVs. Scientists aren't sure why. Some believe that crazy ants like electricity.

Yellow crazy ants eat a leaf beetle.

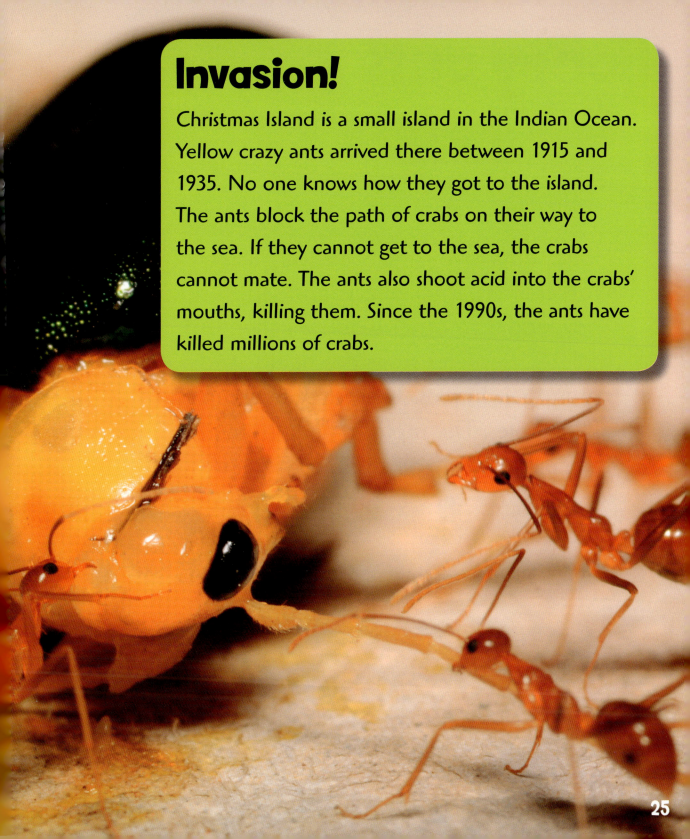

Invasion!

Christmas Island is a small island in the Indian Ocean. Yellow crazy ants arrived there between 1915 and 1935. No one knows how they got to the island. The ants block the path of crabs on their way to the sea. If they cannot get to the sea, the crabs cannot mate. The ants also shoot acid into the crabs' mouths, killing them. Since the 1990s, the ants have killed millions of crabs.

Honey ants

Number of species: about 30
Found: Australia, southern Africa, North America,
    South America and Asia
Length: 0.3 to 1 centimetres (0.1 to 0.4 inches)

Honey ants love to eat sweets. Worker ants gather nectar and sap. They feed it to other workers called repletes. Repletes store the nectar and sap in their bodies. Then they swell up like marbles. The repletes hang from the ceiling of the nest. If another ant is hungry, the replete spits out some of the liquid.

DID YOU KNOW?

Honey ants sometimes kidnap another colony's repletes. They force the repletes to do work.

Army ants

Number of species: more than 300
Found: North and South America, Africa,
       the Middle East, Asia and Australia
Length: 0.3 to 3 centimetres (0.1 to 1.2 inches)

Army ants are some of nature's deadliest hunters. They are also blind. These ants hunt in huge groups, acting like one giant ant. They attack everything in their path. Using large, sharp mandibles, army ants slice into prey. They spray their victims with acid. The acid breaks down the bodies of their prey. The prey becomes easier to eat. Some worker ants carry the prey back to the nest.

DID YOU KNOW?

Army ants hunt in groups of up to 20 million!

In Africa and Asia, army ants are often called driver ants.

Glossary

acid strong liquid

antenna feeler on an insect's head

burrow hole that an animal makes

colony large group of insects or other animals that live together

fungus living thing similar to a plant, but without flowers, leaves or green colouring

larva insect at the stage of development between an egg and an adult

mandible strong mouthparts used to chew

moult shed an outer layer of skin

nectar sweet liquid that some insects collect from flowers and eat as food

predator animal that hunts other animals for food

prey animal that is hunted by another animal for food

pupa insect at the stage of development between a larva and an adult

social living in groups or packs

species group of living things that can reproduce with one another

venom poisonous liquid produced by some animals

Think about ants!

1. Some types of ants live underground. What are some of the benefits of building underground nests? What are some of the drawbacks?

2. Most ant colonies have a single queen. The queen is much larger than her workers. Why do you think the queen is larger? Why do some colonies have more than one queen?

3. Ants live almost everywhere on Earth. How do ants living in warmer habitats differ from ants living in colder habitats? How do their body parts help them to survive?

Find out more

Books

A Colony of Ants: and Other Insect Groups (Animals in Groups), Anna Claybourne (Raintree, 2012)

Amazing Animal Architects Underground, Rebecca Rissman (Raintree, 2018)

Insects (Pocket Eyewitness), DK (DK Children, 2018)

Websites

www.bbc.com/teach/class-clips-video/inside-an-ant-colony/z4crkmn
See inside an ant colony!

www.dkfindout.com/uk/animals-and-nature/insects/ants
Find out more about ants.

Index